Here And Again

David Lawrence

BookLeaf
Publishing

India | USA | UK

Presentation by *BookLeaf Publishing*

Web: www.bookleafpub.com

E-mail: info@bookleafpub.com

ISBN: 9789360946203

First edition 2024

In dedication to Dorothy Jean Lawrence and Greame Taylor.

PREFACE

I sadly suddenly lost my dear mother 14 years ago. It changed me profoundly as ironically I was playing "live forever" on the guitar as she passed away in the other room. Everything I was before as a young man changed in an instant. As if... the heart of her transferred to me. All the knowledge, wisdom, principles and morals she taught me throughout the years that I never took heed to finally became clear. You never know what you have to lose it. You never know Love until you Love someone or something more than yourself. On that fateful day i started to use poetry as my expression of emotions I couldn't comprehend then in time it became my lifes work to become a beacon of Hope to others who in they're darkest days should always remember... Love overcomes all.

Hope

- Hope is a Song note lingering for a While,
Hope is a feeling that Empowers a smile.
- Hope is Serenity when all else fails,
Hope carries across the Oceans with its
wind-swept sails.
- Hope is the Sunrise when you open your Eyes,
Hope will shelter you from your Fear when the
Night raises it's dark-felt ties.
- Hope speaks a promise that One day we'll all
be together high up in the Clouds,
Hope restores Faith in Humanity and a Hero to
Rise amongst the crowd.
- Hope is within all of us,
Hope never requires a Key,
All Hope asks of us is that you Believe in
yourself and Fulfill your Destiny... what your
Born to be.

Dedicated to my old friends high above and
anybody struggling. Stay strong and hold on.
Tomorrow is always a new day x

Fire + Brimstone

- If you had the chance to make a Difference
what would you do?
Sit back on the Sidelines as your mind tells you
one thing but your Heart knows thats not you.
- Through the Fire and Brimstone, the Wind and
the Rain I'm always constantly surprised how
resilient people are when staring Face to Face
with pain.
- From the quiet voice of a woman being abused,
To a child contemplating suffering tormenting
himself saying I've nothing left to lose.
- Clawing away at Humanity these times have
caught us all off guard mouths open wide,
We all thought this couldn't happen to me as Life
shows her ugly side.
- More now than ever it falls upon the Light
from Our hearts,
To remind us why we're here for no one should
Suffer in the Dark.
- If you had the chance to make a Difference
what would You do....
Its never easy i know but atleast promise
yourself that you'll see it Through.

To You

- I mastered my talent throughout the years and the key was you,
As my destiny lies in not only 1 Life it will always be 2.
- There are days when I still Miss you,
The mere Mention of a thought brings all time to a still,
Random memories popping by of You staring at the world just outside over the window sill.
- I grew up never to see you Grow Old,
I experienced moments in life missing out sharing all the stories to be told.
- I Dream because you taught me to Believe,
I love for that was what was shown,
I embrace the Shine in Ones eyes for that was always what greeted me when I came Home.
- As Time rolls on,
Another Year on the books,
Gets harder to remember your voice but God damn I was blessed with your Beautiful looks.
- And so we come to the end Dear Mum,
Who would I be not to shout to the world to once again remember your name,
Dorothy she was called..

Happy Birthday, I love you, I pray these words reach you wherever you now remain.

The Gift

- The Gift that was given to me so Long ago,
Gave me the power to change Lifes and Help others grow.
- This Gift I have earned with living each day of my life,
This Gift which is so Special and Rare,
It makes me Believe inside.
- The simple words of a Human can bring tears of Joy or a Smile,
Simple words that have been spoken will linger for a while.
- It's not the hardest achievement Man has accomplished or the darkest deeds they have forsaken but I truly believe every word I have ever spoken.
- It brings my Night to a close,
The Sun to my rise,
It Breathes life to my Soul and guides my weary eye's.
- I am Grateful and Honoured to have this Gift within me...
Knowing that this Gift will stay for all of Eternity.

Harmony

- A drop In the Ocean creates Ripples they say,
Like Smoke arising from a warm crackling
Fire...
They never Forever stay.
- As If God calls upon Them to come back
Home,
To live out there existence in the place they
Belong.
- In that Moment their Born,
Their Beauty is some sight,
To catch a glimpse of them In their Element is
Our God Given right.
- One of those Times when all Life stands still,
Your Heart slows down and Tears may build.
- The Elegance of Life and Purity it creates,
Has the Power to bring Nations to they're
knees... For all their mistakes.
- Time may have forgotten them,
But in our Hearts they stay True,
As Bright as the sky when it is so gracefully
blue.
- Everything has a Beginning
Everything had an End,
But in that Moment of Harmony...
Maybe we could call them Our Friend.

Serenity

- A Whispering wind,
The Sands of Time,
Lost Memories of the Past which have been left
behind.
- The Rising Sun,
Which brings new Hope to You,
Warms even the coldest Hearts to All but a Few.
- Serenity, Serendipity, Harmony and More,
Restores Faith to the Broken and brings them
Joy galore.
- The soft breeze in a summers morning,
The calmness of the Air,
You just sometimes Close your Eyes and Know
something else is there.
- The Heart may skip a beat,
You May look up for a glance,
When all the Pieces just Fit and the Clouds
begin to Dance.
- It's Easy to Believe,
It's Harder to keep that Belief True,
But it is rather rewarding when that Peaceful
Moment Happens to You.

Life-Force

- There was a Time when My Heart was so
Strong,
Beating at the right pace,
Never Leading Me Wrong.
- It gave me Strength,
It gave me Power,
Helping Me to stand as Tall as a Tower.
- My Mother's Heart was Pure but frail,
The day She passed it sadly failed.
- I Never dreamt My fate would be like that,
Until my Heart began to race and Light turned
Dark.
- Faster and Faster...
Oh Help Me My Lord,
Skipping the beats like a Broken guitar chord.
- The Air was My Friend,
But Now an Enemy it is,
With Every Breath I took,
The Life draining from Me like Bubbles from a
fizz.
- I Never saw that White Glistening Light,
That supposedly occurs when Your day turns to
Night.
- I Never had flashbacks of Times gone by,

I Never had those questions run through My
head, When, Who or Why.
- I Never shed a Tear,
Or Cried out in Pain,
But the Thought crossed my mind that I would
see You again.
- It Must not be My Time,
Not My Time to go,
For I Am still here writing this...
For You All To Know.

Rise Again

- From the Ashes I may Rise,
All of Your Blessings in Disguise.
- The power of Grace from Above,
Filling each and every one of Us with countless
years of Love.
- The spark that may have Gone,
Past away,
Returns with a Vengeance to lead you into the
Fray.
- My Soul cleansed,
My Belief renewed,
A Lifetime of mistakes written out of the
passages from that Druid.
- That Oak tree I envisioned,
Once withered from Life,
Suddenly bursts into colour with the Birds
singing You will be allright.
- The Fire that for so long consumed me,
That burnt everything I may have touched was
replaced with something else,
So that I may Tell the World Your Lord Loves
You So Much.
- Faith may just be a word,
But the Meanings in the Heart,

Just hold Your hands up and ask Him to take you
back to the start.
- The World He will show you,
Will Open up Your eyes,
Turning You away from all the Darkness and
Lies.
- Out of the Ashes I may Rise again...
My Lord,
My Friend.

Scotland

- The country I Love,
The country where I was Born,
The Land of the Free,
The Land of the ever-green and Thistle thorn.
- For aslong as Time has existed we have Stood
Courageous and True,
Our Flag swirling gracefully in the autumn's
wind, White and Blue.
- Our country may be Small,
But Passionately Our Kinsmen are,
Never surrendering to countries who are so 'a'
far.
- Like Brick to Brick,
We have Stood Together against the tides,
Wave after Wave,
Never giving up inside.
- To not Stand on Our own two feet is like
admitting defeat,
Throwing away the memories of Our Selfless
fallen who Fought to give Us this land so We
may eat.
- The Time may come again,
When We will have to Rise my Friends,
To Fulfill Our Destiny... "Ya get me ya Ken"

The Streets

- Destiny has a way of choosing Someone's path,
And the Desicions One makes may come full
circle that They feel its Wrath.
- We can All be dealt bad cards in Life,
The Aces hid away,
And Ones Journey turns from Happiness to
Plight.
- Maybe They caused Their own downfall,
Maybe Fate intervened,
But maybe Time simply ran out for Them to
follow Their Dreams.
- The struggle for Survival and the sense of
Dread that it brings,
Leaves the Essence of Life in the balance,
Balance as a Pendulum swings.
- I truly Believe it is Our duty as a human being
to support One another,
Regardless of Faith, Creed or even Colour.
- I to Myself,
Have caused the destruction of my own Life,
I to Myself,
Have broken the Boundaries between Wrong
and Right.
- It is easy to Forget that aslong as Their Heart
beats They are still alive,

The Pain is Real,
As Hope diminishes from Their Weary eyes.
- My Prayer to You,
Is No matter what has happened,
Or is to come,
Compassion and Hope is Always there,
For I am thinking about All of You,
You Will Always be Someone.

Greame

- And so we layed Our Friend down to Sleep,
The Stars converged and families weeped.
- Friends reunited,
The world coming as One,
Bowing our head in Dedication for you were
always as bright as the Sun.
- I Pray for your Peace every Night and every
Day and desperately hoping for the light to
switch off as a sign that I know your ok.
- I hold my Heart, Heavy and True, but seeing
the Love today for You will always get me
through.
- And as your favourite song Slide played and
the curtains were Closed....
I closed my eyes and said thank you my friend....
But death is but a Journey we all must behold.

My Dear Friend

- Gresh... Its been 3 months now since you Grew
Your Wings,
Going to meet Boyce Avenue in November and
I'll be telling Them how much You use to Love
them sing.
- I can't speak for Everyone but I Believe for this
We can All be as one,
From Distant Friend to Dear Brother we all Miss
you and Pray your settled amongst the morning
Sun.
- Just like Mum,
I never remembered to say the things I had to
Before I ran out of Time,
But I Truly Believe your around us all giving
Subtle Signs.
- A phrase stumbled across me last week "We're
all born with wings some just grow theirs sooner
than others",
And when you Fell asleep yours Emerged with a
Heavenly flutter.
- From an Old Friend,
When a Friendship became intertwined,
My Words are My Heart until the End of Time.

Faith

- Faith... What can I say,
The Word that echoes through my Heart and
Soul every Minute of every Day.
-Through Times of Hardship,
And Moments of Joy,
For 8 Years I've been seeking the answers going
back to when I was a Boy.
- In my Darkest Days that would Freeze even the
Warmest Heart,
In My Bleakest seconds when my Life was
falling Apart.
- Crumbling to my knees with my eyes aimed to
the Heavens pouring out with Dispair,
Pleading for the Answers my Heart truly needed
to Hear.
- Sometimes I felt comfort,
Sometimes I felt wings Wrapping me in Love,
But I Dread the occasions where there's been No
reply from High Above.
- They say God Always listens,
But sometimes He leaves mountains unmoved
that Road set before you Always gives You
something to prove.
- And after many Battles Won,
And countless Battles Lost,

Faith is simply a Promise of Hope,
For Hope is worth Believing in no matter the
Struggle or Cost.

Mum

- There's a place I know where Darkness turns to Light, for when those times appear I simply close My eyes and everything just for a second becomes O so so Bright.
- I still Hope,
I still Believe and Pray,
That the God I have Faith in will grant me the chance to once again see You someday.
- I Struggle to spread your Ashes,
To me that means the final link to my Friend is broken,
I still try to open my Heart up to the wise Words you once had spoken.
- For every Year that goes by,
For every Day that passes when you are not here,
For every Darkest night I face your Star still shines bright calling to me reminding me why I'm still Here.
- Everybody deserves a second chance in Life, But Yours has already begun, Shooting across the night sky in a Blaze of Glory for you Mum......
You my dear Mum will always be my Number One.

Christmas Angels

-It's that Time of the Year again,
That Time of Year,
When the world is Illuminated with Light and
the Magic of Christmas is carried with Hopeful
cheer.
-I use the One Gift bestowed upon me from a
Mothers Love,
To give Homage to Our Dearly departed residing
High, so High above.
-The meaning of Christmas was born from a
Saint,
Kindness, Hope, Compassion and a Love that
centuries could never ever taint.
-We've all lost Friends, Family, Loved ones we
cherished Dear,
This Time of Year can be especially hard for we
long to have them Here..
But please Remember the Meaning of Christmas
gives us a smile because when we close our eyes
they're love is Always Near.
-And as I raise a glass...
And as I let my Heart sing...
I Bow my head and Thank them...
I Thank them for memories only Heroes can
bring.

9 Years A Hero

-On this Fateful Day many moons ago,
God took back one of his most precious Stones,
But time has not forgotten that moment you had
to leave Home.
-It's rained, it's snowed, at times its been ever so
bitterly cold...
But Love binds us together no matter where in
the Heavens you now sit upon your Throne.
-Your pictures still radiant Warmth,
Our memories live on Day to Day,
My Blessing for Poetry comes only because you
told me there was a Different side I should
Embrace.
-I always picture you amongst the Evergreens,
Sadly though for now just out of my Sight,
In a Land over the horizon simply basking in a
pure Glistening perfect Light.
-Time is a great Healer,
And all these years you've missed will make our
Greatest chat,
But for now I'm signing off Mum though always
remember Thank you..
Thank you for the Best Friend a Son could ever
have.

Sinners + Saints

-In a World rife and controlled by Fear,
Where do you draw the line between Sacrifice
and untold tears?
- So many Soul's,
But so much Hate,
It's easier to be a Sinner,
Than it is to be a Saint.
-Where's the Understanding, Kindness,
Compassion, Empathy and Love..
As you walk by someone with those eyes and
right away start to judge.
-An Angel isn't someone born with Entitlement
or blessed with untold Gold,
It is a Heart in pure flight,
Their reward is your Joy,
And Joy is something they Dearly keep close.
-They walk among us even if,
Even if they are few,
But always there in the shadows waiting,
Waiting to catch You.
-An Angel in disguise,
Comes in all Shapes and Sizes,
In a world eaiser to be a Sinner than a Saint,
Angel's are Always near,
Always over your shoulder lieing in wait.

Once Upon A Time

- Once upon a Time when Autumn shut up shop,
And the Leaves that lay on the ground retired
Peacefully for the Season's never stop.
- Their was a Boy who knew it was that Time of
Year again,
That Time of the Year,
When Santa dusted down his Old sleigh to fulfil
Children's wishes,
Spread some Magical Christmas cheer.
- When the days turned into Nights,
When His excitement grew intense,
Wondering if this Year had He been good
enough for Santa to bring his Favourite present.
- Now the Frosty mornings and Chilly breezes
didn't shake his Belief,
That Santa was visiting his Home but He knew
to Remember to leave a glass of Milk and some
Cookies for Him to eat.
- Rushing home from school,
Slipping on the ice He felt like a fool,
But that evening the Christmas tree went up and
that moment was Always memorable.
- What colour of Lights...
A Star or Angel for the top...
It was Always a Happy Time,

All night the Smiles never stopped.
- And so Here we Are,
Christmas Eve,
Christmas Day is so very near,
He struggles to get to sleep breathing quietly so
He might know when Santa was finally Here.
- He must of been tired,
For before He knew it the Time had finally
come,
He awoke with His Mum calling "David Santas
been, come see what He's left you Son".
- Darting out of bed in an instant,
He couldn't contain His delight,
Santa had brought His Wish and Oh my it was a
Beautiful sight.
- Once upon a time Their was a Boy...
Who was very grateful to Santa that Year for
bringing His Favourite Toy.

Above All Else

-As I Draw closer to the End of My life,
I've started to pay more attention to some of
Gods Heavenly Sights.
- Its Never Easy losing someone close,
Or a Dear Friend you Loved,
I take Comfort in a Promise that One Day We'll
All meet again Above.
- I imagine Them being a shooting Star on a
calm Autumn night,
Or a Gentle breeze caressing My face to let me
know Their alright.
- I would like to Believe the Dreams They once
had,
But Never had the Time to fulfil,
Doesn't leave with Them as One Day Hope will
come calling to use Them still.
- And Here I Am,
Sitting here Gazing out of the window watching
the World fly by,
Writing down My Legacy reminding the World,
Above All Else...
True Love Never Dies.

Gone To Soon

- You never know Love,
Until you Love something more than Yourself.
And by God it stings like an ever lasting skelf.
- I Lost a Child,
Truthfully it was Us Both,
The Tears never ending...
A Forever filling moat
- It wasn't the First Time,
Second or even Third,
As a Christian it brought me to my Knees more
times with the Hurt.
- You question Yourself,
You point your rage at God,
As Your Prayers go unanswered Your Faith is all
you've got.
- The Thoughts of Ending it All,
Comes and Goes at Times,
But I know if I Leave it will be an Eternal over
lapping Rhyme.
- Life can be a cruel Mistress,
What Your Purpose, Belief, Faith in is Yours
alone,
But Theres Nothing more Depressing when You
Live a Life that's not Your Home.
- My Purpose though...

Is to be Here until the End,
Fighting for the Meek and Lonely Always,
Always being Their Friend.
- My little Sam,
All of the Angels I never got to Knew,
Your Father Is walking In your Name,
Name For You.

Here And Back Again

- 14 years of writing has it finally came to this,
When the end of an era has been reached,
Doors finally closed forever I've made it I can
now be at peace.
- A promise,
An endeavour,
My wish carried upon many a prayer...
Looking back through all my old writing's I am
so very thankful I'm not back there.
- This journey has been a Hard one,
To be honest I'm surprised I've gotten this Far,
But seeing how I wrote "Hope" back in 2012 it
does prove something resides above in the Stars.
- The Pain...
Oh the Pain can never truly go away...
Though Love...
Though Love will Always stay.
- As personal as one can get you've had a
glimpse into a Soul that only God can really
feel,
I honestly appreciate you taking this journey
with me even sometimes amongst Satan's
battlefield.
- I have nothing to Prove anymore...

But maybe I do because Eternity lasts forever my age old quest for answers showed me I'm upto the task.

- I've had to relive old wounds,

I've had to dust off the drawers that I kept so closely guarded at bay to finish this book off so oh my what an experience it was to fall back into the darkness once again...

And Once again my Angels came down to save me.

- I've never wrote for money,

Money or Pride,

I simply wrote Emotion...

Emotion will always make you stronger how you choose to release it is for you to decide.

- Now I take my leave now,

I bid you farewell and Wish you all the Best,

Here And Back Again this chapter is finished...

I made it Mum I Hope I've made you proud your Boy has passed Redemption's test.

#OneLove xXx

Milton Keynes UK
Ingram Content Group UK Ltd.
UKHW022333230424
441619UK00015B/764

9 789360 946203